NORTHUMBERLAND
IN WATERCOLOUR II

Illustrated by DAPHNE HARRISON

Written by JOHN TAYLOR

ANSIS PUBLISHING

Created from an original idea by Daphne Harrison

CHILLINGHAM FROM ROS CASTLE

With thanks to Kerr McGee Oil who supported
the publication of this book.

Text © 2000 John Taylor
Illustrations © 2000 Daphne Harrison
Edited text, design and layout © 2000 Ansis Publishing
First published in 2000 by Ansis Publishing, Estate Office,
Alnwick Castle, Alnwick, Northumberland NE66 ING

Design: Mick Hodson Associates

ISBN 0-9519529-2-7

Printed in China

Contents

R Tweed
•BERWICK

•FORD

FLODDEN
FIELD

COLDSTREAM •

•ETAL

BRANXTON •

R Tweed

R. Till

LINDISFARNE

ROSS•
BUDLE BAY

North Sea

R. Glen

WOOLER •

•CHILLINGHAM

R. Breamish

•ALNWICK

•ESLINGTON

WHITTINGHAM •
•LEMMINGTON HALL

•ALNHAM

CALLALY •

•EDLINGHAM

BIDDLESTONE•
CLENNEL

•ALWINTON

HARBOTTLE •

•CRAGSIDE

R. Coquet

•ELSDON

•NUNNYKIRK

FOREWORD

Many people have a blinkered view of Northumberland as a county blighted by an industrial past. Nothing could be further from the truth, and this book shows some of the less well-known treasures of a beautiful county, together with its folklore and traditions.

Daphne Harrison's snapshots in paint, and John Taylor's tales from the past combine to enthuse the reader with a genuine and enjoyable taste of a little-known area of England.

THE DUKE OF NORTHUMBERLAND

AUTHOR'S NOTE

Many of the tales in this book come from Northumberland's rich store of folklore, the oral tradition that is related and handed down over the cottage hearth or in the village inn. Most of us in Northumberland are very close to our roots and our history, whether it be from castle or cottage. I hope that readers enjoy these parts of Northumberland as much as Daphne Harrison and I did during our research.

JOHN TAYLOR

CHAPTER ONE

BELSAY

ELSAY IS the creation of one family, the Middletons, whose home it was for over 700 years. It is a perfect example of the development and history of rural Northumberland. The first member of the Middleton family recorded as owning Belsay - and strangely enough the only member to achieve national prominence - was Sir Richard de Middleton, King Henry III's Lord Chancellor from 1269 until 1272, when the King died. After Sir Richard the family retreated into domesticity and followed the usual rural pursuits, including a little banditry. Some members of the family kidnapped two cardinals who were on a diplomatic mission to Scotland at the time of the Border wars, later paying for this with their lives.

Belsay Castle originated as a fortified tower during the 14th century and reflected the troubled state of those times, when there was the constant threat of an invasion from Scotland while England's attention was focussed on the 100 Years' War with France. The later addition of the unfortified wing in 1614, after the union of the crowns under James I and VI, mirrored the coming of a more settled state of civil affairs in this part of Northumberland. It was around this time that the Middleton family baronetcy came into being. James I raised money by allowing landowners of a certain status to request elevation to the title of baronet, which is hereditary but not part of the peerage, in return for a sizeable payment.

Belsay Castle, Hall and Stables

Belsay Hall (which is completely separate from the old Belsay Castle) and the present layout of the estate is principally the work of three men. Sir William Middleton (1738-1795) 5th Bart, began the process by diverting roads in the vicinity and enclosing parkland and farms. Sir Charles Middleton (1779-1867) 6th Bart, was responsible for building the present Hall and appurtenances, and creating the beautiful 'quarry' garden. Around 1800 he inherited an estate in Lincolnshire from his maternal grandfather and had to change his name to Monck under the terms of the will. Sir Arthur Middleton (1867-1933) 7th Bart, resumed the family name in 1876, and was responsible for developing the farms on the estate, constructing many farm buildings and houses.

The Hall at Belsay was designed and built by Sir Charles, 6th Bart, following a leisurely honeymoon combined with a grand tour of Europe, from September 1804 to April 1806 at the height of the Napoleonic wars. He visited Denmark, Berlin, Dresden, Prague, Vienna, Trieste and Venice, but it was Greece that influenced Sir Charles most. The great wealth from his estates in Northumberland, Essex and Lincolnshire, developed by prudent management during this period of agricultural expansion, allowed Sir Charles to design and build a country house based on the pure Grecian classical architecture seen during his stay in Athens. He was assisted in his designs by the pioneering archaeologist, Sir William Gell, and some later revisions were carried out by John Dobson of Newcastle.

The plan of this great Greek Revival house is exactly 100 ft square and Sir Charles himself calculated each proportional ratio to three places of decimals. It took around 10 years to complete, using sandstone from a quarry just a few hundred yards away from the house, and within the park.

Belsay Hall Gardens

On completion of the house, Sir Charles created a romantic garden within the quarry. The rest of the landscape and gardens which surround the Hall and Castle were also designed and laid out by Sir Charles Monck in the first half of the 19th century, but the exotic plantings of his son, Sir Arthur Middleton, 7th Bart, introduced more informality. His rhododendrons and many other evergreens, as well as unusual tree species, have all added to the charm of Belsay.

As with many other similar country estates, its prosperity effectively came to an end with the Great War of 1914-18, although the family continued to live here until 1962, surviving a deep agricultural depression, as well as death duties, taxation and the occupation of the house by the military during the Second World War. The core of the surrounding estate is now owned by a charitable trust which will ensure continuing support for the hall, castle and gardens, now controlled and being restored by English Heritage, who have opened up the property to the public.

Belsay Quarry Garden

CHAPTER TWO

WALLINGTON

Fair Wallington has been decreed by Fate
To be the Capital of a Fair Estate

JOHN ADAMSON, '*Cheviot*'

WALLINGTON, WITH its hall and estate, is one of the jewels in the National Trust's vast portfolio of property throughout England. It was given to the Trust by Sir Charles Trevelyan in 1941 subject to his life interest, and on his death in 1958 the National Trust assumed full control of the estate.

Originally, Wallington belonged to a branch of the Fenwick family who inherited it by marriage to a Strother heiress in the 14th century. The property passed by purchase to the Blackett family; that family's fortune being founded by the great merchant

prince of Tyneside, Sir William Blackett. The third son of that gentleman - another Sir William, but now a baronet though also engaged in coal, lead mining and shipping - built the original hall in 1688 and developed the estate. The Wallington of the present time owes much to his endeavours. His drive and imagination is impressed upon the estate and surrounding countryside.

It was one of Sir William's successors, Sir Walter Calverley Blackett, who was responsible for the present outward appearance of the hall as a result of alterations largely completed in 1745. He also did much to adorn the grounds and gardens, employing James Paine to design and construct the bridge over the river Wansbeck to the south of the hall, as well as Daniel Garrett who designed many of the estate farms and did some of the building work on the hall and in the gardens.

Wallington Hall and the 'Griffins' Heads'

Sir Walter also employed Capability Brown, who had lived and worked at the nearby Kirkharle estate as a young man, to design the pleasure grounds at Rothley Lake with its follies, Rothley Castle and the Cadgers Fort, which overlooks this tremendous vista. Brown is also thought to have landscaped the surrounds of Wallington Hall.

The Trevelyans, who were of Cornish origin, inherited the properties of Wallington and Cambo from the Blackett family. They produced artists, civil servants and men and women of letters, who owned and lived at Wallington for nearly 200 years. The interior at Wallington owes much to them. In 1855 John Ruskin, the art critic, advised that the courtyard be roofed over and that William Bell Scott, a young Newcastle artist, be commissioned to paint on its walls a series of pictures illustrating Northumbrian history - the Descent of the Danes, the Death of Bede, Grace Darling, etc - culminating in a glorification of 'iron and coal'.

Sir Charles Trevelyan, 3rd Baronet, who gave the property to the National Trust, was a Liberal MP for 30 years, then a Socialist MP. He was President of the Board of Education in Ramsay MacDonald's first Labour Government in 1924, and again in MacDonald's National Government from 1929-1931. In 1930, he was appointed Lord Lieutenant of Northumberland, which proved to be very unpopular locally, though he held the post until his death in 1958. In 1946 some students offended him by painting the 'Griffins' Heads' from the original 'Bishops Gate' in London (which had been brought north by Sir Walter Blackett in one of his collier ships in 1760) on the east lawn of the house, bright red, as well as painting a crown on one of his gate pillars, and a hammer and sickle on the other, presumably in honour of his political affiliations.

Wallington Hall and its gardens and grounds are now open to the public, and the estate is managed by the National Trust as part of the endowment supporting the Hall and its contents.

The Wansbeck sings with all her springs,
The bents and braes give ear

A.C. SWINBURNE, *'A Jacobite's Exile'*

Wallington Lake

Wallington Hall Gardens

Cadgers Fort and Rothley Castle

CHAPTER THREE

NUNNYKIRK

NUNNYKIRK HALL is a classical Dobson mansion, designed and built by the well-known Newcastle architect in 1825 for William Orde, the squire of Nunnykirk, on the site of an earlier house, and indeed incorporating elements of it. The Orde family, who still own the property, have held lands in Northumberland and Durham for centuries, providing magistrates and deputy lieutenants for the county of Northumberland, as well as an Admiral of the Blue Squadron, and an MP. The Hall is now used by a charity as a school for children with dyslexic and associated problems.

William Orde is probably best known for his horse-racing and horse-breeding exploits. 'Tomboy' carried his racing colours of white with dark blue sleeves and dark blue cap to victory, winning the first Northumberland Plate run on Newcastle Town Moor in 1833. He owned and bred the celebrated mare, 'Beeswing'. She was sired by Dr Syntax, a horse bred by Squire Riddell of Felton Park, another celebrated owner and breeder who won 17 gold cups during his racing career. One of Riddell's horses - with the curious name of XYZ - alone won nine gold cups.

Nunnykirk Hall

River Font

'Beeswing' had a remarkable career on the turf, winning 51 races and 21 gold cups before retiring in 1842. After having eight foals (four colts and four fillies, several of whom were winners on the turf), the 'pride of the north' died on 4th March 1854 near Chester aged 21 years. 'Beeswing' acquired her name in interesting circumstances. The two squires were enjoying a glass of port together when Mr Orde was told about the birth of the bay filly. Squire Riddell, reflecting on the bees which were buzzing around their glasses at that time, suggested the name to his friend who readily agreed. Once 'Beeswing' was a common name on many an inn sign in the north, rivalling the Marquis of Granby or Lord Nelson.

CHAPTER FOUR

CRAGSIDE

CRAGSIDE HOUSE and grounds, now a property of the National Trust, were the creation of one man, Lord Armstrong of Cragside, the great industrialist and armaments king who, virtually single-handed, also created industrial Tyneside. As a young solicitor, Armstrong took an interest in science, and claimed he came back frequently to Rothbury, 'for the fishing, mostly', though the river must have steered him towards the study of hydraulics. In 1847 he set up an engineering works specializing in this field.

Following the Crimean War, when the failings of Great Britain's hopelessly out-of-date army - especially its weaponry, its organisation and its support arrangements - became exposed to public scrutiny, William Armstrong started to take an interest in gunnery. The Armstrong Gun which emerged was breech- instead of muzzle-loaded, fired a shell rather than a cannon ball, had a rifled barrel rather than a smooth one, and was made from steel, not cast iron. He gave the patents for these new inventions to the government. He was appointed Master of the Ordnance and received his knighthood and the Order of the Companion of the Bath for these services.

Armstrong organised and developed the Whittle Dene waterworks, and used hydraulic power to improve the cranes on Tyneside for dockside and industrial use. By 1863, he had formed his own cranage company, and had created his first company

works at Elswick. He was by now a very wealthy man. In 1868 he launched his first gunboat, and another yard on the Tyne was opened to build warships for the Admiralty and other foreign governments. The very gun that he had invented stimulated demand for armour-plated iron-clads, which he now met. In 1884 he opened a steelworks and, at the time of his death in 1900, the total works covered 230 acres and employed 25,000 men. Lord Armstrong of Cragside, as he became three years before his death in 1900, was a figure comparable to Alfred Krupp in Germany and Andrew Carnegie in the United States.

Tumbleton Lake

For his relaxation, he leased 411 acres of land at Cragside from the 4th Duke of Northumberland in 1863 for a term of 60 years. On this steep piece of moor he built his first house. By 1873 he had purchased the freehold of this leased ground for £4,840 in order to build the mansion of Cragside as we know it, which was designed by Norman Shaw with much Tudor half-timbering far removed from anything found in Northumbrian vernacular building styles. In 1882 he extended his estate by purchasing from the Duke a further 2,165 acres of the Snitter Estate (Rothbury Demense and West Debdon) at a notional cost of £21,600, yielding a rental of £497 per annum. In fact Armstrong ended up by exchanging Wooden and Buston Farms, which he had just bought valued at £20,000 at a rental of £834, with the Duke instead. Some 2,339 acres of land at Cragend Farm, Debdon Whitefield and West Newton Farm were also purchased from the 7th Duke, costing £18,600 and yielding a rental of £493 per annum. In all, these lands were valued at 33½ years' purchase on the rents. These transactions were the beginning of the Cragside estate at Rothbury.

Lord Armstrong also added to his estate at Cragside by purchasing from other neighbouring landowners until he owned most of the land from Rothbury to Warton along the Coquetside and as far to the north-west as Netherton; in all, he bought approximately 20,000 acres surrounding Cragside. He planted millions of trees, seven million in the 1,729 acres of Cragside's pleasure grounds alone together with countless rhododendrons, constructed several lakes and miles of private drives. The lakes provided the water supply to power the turbines which provided the electricity for Cragside, the first house in the kingdom to be so lit. Armstrong also rebuilt all of the farmhouses, cottages and steadings right across his estate. It could truly be said that the motto below the mantelpiece in the dining-room at Cragside, 'East or west - hame's best', is how he viewed his home and his estate, though it did not prevent him from also purchasing Bamburgh Castle.

Cragside

Some time in the 1860s a young man from Whittingham came to the village of Rothbury to look after one of his father's (and uncle's) shops; his name was David Dippie Dixon. A small, shy, kindly man, his job was to travel throughout Upper Coquetdale taking orders and delivering goods to his father's customers. His interest in the history and natural history of Coquetdale and neighbouring Whittingham Vale caused him to collect and file data on these subjects and, over the years, he contributed articles to various scientific and historical publications. In time, the family business closed down. Fortunately Lord Armstrong, who had been impressed by this young man, offered him a job looking after the archives and the library at Cragside. Here Dixon spent the rest of his life, during which time he wrote his celebrated books, *Whittingham Vale* and *Upper Coquetdate*. These were the best detailed local histories of these areas until the 'Northumberland County History' volumes were published. David Dippie Dixon was born in 1842 and died at Cragend, in a home provided by the Armstrong family, in 1929.

Cragside Grounds

CHAPTER FIVE

CALLALY

CALLALY WAS, for over 500 years, the home of the Clavering family. It claimed descent from the family of Fitz-Roger, Lords of Warkworth, who bought the manor from a Jew of York, who held the mortgage of the last Saxon owners. The main branch of the Claverings of Warkworth died out in 1332, but a cadet branch held Callaly from then until 1877, when the estate and castle were sold to Alexander H Browne of Doxford.

An old tradition tells of a difference of opinion between the lord and his lady over the siting of Callaly Castle. The lord wished to rebuild on Castle Hill; his lady disagreed, preferring a more secluded site on Shepherd's Shaw. The lady disguised one of her servants as a monster boar and directed him to demolish the building work on the Castle Hill site. The lord sent his servants to guard the site after work finished in the evening, and the appearance of the monster drove them to flee in terror. So the castle was finally built on Shepherd's Shaw. A medieval tower forms the south-west angle of the present building, which is largely 17th and 18th century. Inside, there is plaster work from 1750 by the same team of Italians who worked at Wallington. The children of Whittingham school, certainly until recently, used to recite this piece of folklore:

> *Callaly Castle built on the height,*
> *Up i' the day an' doon i' the night;*
> *If ye build it on Shepherd's Shaw*
> *There it'll stand an' never fa'.*

Callaly Castle and Stables

On the eastern side of the park at Callaly is a very ancient stone wall. No one knows its date or provenance, but it has always been regarded locally as the ancient boundary between the Whittingham and Callaly estates.

The Claverings were a papist family and held to their faith over the centuries, supporting a priest at Callaly during the turbulent times following the Reformation. Callaly Castle was sequestered by Cromwell - but returned by Charles II. Later the Claverings supported the Jacobites. Following the death of the last Clavering (John Edward in 1881) the Catholics worshipped in the new church of St Mary Immaculate - on a site (reputedly a bog) given by the Ravensworth family - midway between Glanton and Whittingham. The last Clavering to be associated with Callaly was the late Major Clavering of the Essex branch of the family, who commanded the Warkworth and Shilbottle company of the Home Guard in World War II. This included a section based at Whittingham and Callaly.

With the advent of the Browne family, the castle and the estate farms were improved and developed. Major Alex Browne of Callaly was known as the 'Cock of the North' among his contemporaries in High Leicestershire where he used to take a train load

of horses every hunting season. One of his most notable horses was 'Silvertop', a grey - capable of leaping everything and anything - which ran in the Grand National. For many years Major Alex used to invite friends and neighbours to hunt over his land; his staff had instructions to padlock all of the gates in order to force his guests to jump over them or the fences if they wanted to follow his hounds.

Locals in the vale have a weather tradition: 'If Callaly Pot boils in the summer, rain is on its way.' Callaly Pot is the area of ground between Howlet's Haa' and Castle Hill; it is a deep hollow surrounded by dense, mature woodland and dense undergrowth. In early morning or late evening in summer the mist rises from this area and it is said that 'Callaly Pot is steaming'.

Callaly Castle and Grounds

CHAPTER SIX

WHITTINGHAM VALE

WHITTINGHAM VALE is the colloquial name for the upper reaches of the River Aln. Its nickname, until recent times, was 'Whisky Valley', due, no doubt, to the habits of the locals. The whisky was originally supplied by Messrs Dixon of Whittingham in grey, gallon jars called 'Grey Hens' and gave the Vale an unrivalled reputation for generous hospitality. The Vale, as it is known by its inhabitants, stretches from the ducal park walls at Brizlee to the source of the river Aln at Alnham. First mentioned by the Greek writer Ptolemy of Alexandria as the river 'Aulauna', the river meanders its way the length of the valley, draining and watering an area of fertile farmland. The vale contains several parishes, the chief of which is Whittingham. Generally regarded as the centre of a group of Anglian settlements, the village is believed to have been the site of an important synod held in 664AD and instrumental in choosing St Cuthbert as Bishop of Lindisfarne.

For centuries some of the parishes of the area were held under terms of 'Drengage' (a form of feudal service to Bamburgh Castle), some under terms of 'Truncage' (to supply logs to Bamburgh Castle on given dates), while some had to supply men and materials to the King's war-bands. Latterly the manors were held by Herons, Fenwicks, Collingwoods, Alders and Claverings. Plague visited the area regularly and the 'lost' villages of Barton and Abberwick are believed to have been the victims of this pestilence which arrived in 1349. On the other hand Border strife may have played a part in their disappearance as neither site is recorded as having pele towers or any defensive structures.

Whittingham Vale

Modern Whittingham can generally be regarded as commencing after 1719 when the Liddell family (Earls and Barons of Ravensworth in Co Durham) purchased the village and farms in the parish. This wealthy coal-owning family improved and developed their estates and the village. Many of the farmhouses, cottages, farm steadings and field shapes date from after their arrival. The village inn with the neighbouring Castle Farm was originally the coaching inn (where the Edinburgh-bound coach called late morning and the Newcastle-bound coach called late afternoon) before the days of the realignment of the A697 as a turnpike road in 1849, when the Bridge of Aln Hotel replaced them, only to be superseded by the coming of the Railway.

The ancient pele tower, which originally belonged to the Heron family, was converted in 1845 to a workhouse for the impoverished elderly by the Liddell family. There are three fountains in the village which formerly supplied clean drinking water and which also serve as memorials; the most interesting is in the centre of the village, erected to commemorate Athole, 3rd Earl of Ravensworth who was fondly regarded by the inhabitants. He contemplates his village with his stick in his hand, his plaid over his shoulder and his faithful collie at his feet, carved in stone forever. Shops in the village used to supply most of the local needs; Dixon's shop was the family business of David Dippie Dixon (see p 26) supplying provisions and the famous 'Grey Hens': the Ewart family supplied the drapery needs of the district and the Scotts were, for many years, the district butchers. All of these shops are now dwellings.

Whittingham Vale has, until recently, been regarded as one of the prime stockrearing and feeding areas in Northumberland. For many years a fair was held here on St Bartholomew's day. Before the advent of the local auction mart, large numbers of cattle were sold, among all the other 'fun of the fair'. With the demise of the cattle sales, the fair developed into the Whittingham Athletic Games and, for more than a century, was one of the premier athletic events in Northumberland and the Borders. Sadly these games no longer exist, but the village flower and sheep show still carries on. The 'Latter Fair', which is a hangover from the original fair, is held on the Monday evening following the village show and is for the benefit of the local children.

> If ever ye gan tae Whittingham Fair,
> Be sure and caa at the 'Hole-i-the-Waa'
> For there ye'll get whisky for nowt,
> An brandy for naethin at-aa.

> (The Hole-In-The-Wall Cottage is an old public house.)

Eslington Park and the Lady's Bridge

An amusing, but true, tale concerns a one-time treasurer of Whittingham Athletic Games who had to report to his Annual Meeting that all of the paper work, including a number of cheques and notes relating to the previous Games, had been destroyed by a mouse in his rolltop desk. This transparently honest man produced the shredded paper as evidence and his word was readily accepted - but with some regret! At Eslington, the Liddell family built the present Eslington Park, around 1720. The route of the original drive to old Eslington crosses the 'Lady's Bridge', one of the oldest bridges in the county; privately built and privately owned, the heaviest traffic now carried is tractors and trailers. Eslington was a Collingwood residence and manor prior to 1719. Famously it was the home of the redoubtable Sir Cuthbert Collingwood who was taken prisoner at the battle of Reidswire by the Scots in 1575 but then ransomed. In 1587 the 'Bold Buccleuch' ran a foray down Aln water and stormed Eslington, to Sir Cuthbert's great embarrassment and disadvantage, capturing his son and lifting most of his livestock. The last Collingwood of Eslington supported the Earl of Derwentwater and the Jacobite cause in 1715, for which he lost his head on Tower Hill. There is a Border verse playing on the coat of arms of the Collingwoods and the Scotts of Buccleugh, which features the head of a roebuck in a bush:

Since in the bush the buck was ta'en;
But when the bush shall hold the buck,
Then farewell faith, and farewell luck.

Among the many characters who have lived in Whittingham Vale over the years probably one of the most interesting was John Henry Rogerson of Rothill. Originally the village blacksmith, he kept some cattle and sheep on a few rented fields near the village prior to the Great War. After the war ended, he rented the large farm of Rothill from the Eslington estate. When the great depression hit farming some years later, and a large section of that estate was sold, he bought the farm. He was, by the time of his demise, highly regarded locally as a very successful farmer and extremely popular. He was also a good horseman and his great friend was the neighbouring squire, Major Alex Browne of Callaly Castle (see p 30), who admired his courage and horsemanship. Unfortunately they fell out one day over a trivial matter, and the hot-tempered squire blasted Rogerson saying, 'You were just a blacksmith, now become a farmer', to which Rogerson retorted, 'If you had been born a blacksmith, you would still be a blacksmith, and a damned bad 'un'. Sad to say, they never spoke to each other again, but often expressed regret over the exchange to others.

CHAPTER SEVEN

BIDDLESTONE

Biddlestone was long the seat of the Selby family. The township was one of the 10 towns of Coquetdale which owed suit and service to Harbottle Castle during the Middle Ages: Biddlestone, Clennel, Chirmundsden, Sharperton, Farnham, Burradon, Netherton and, strangely enough, Fawdon and Ingram in the Breamish some way to the north. Following the Conquest and the spread of Norman influence, these towns formed part of the barony of the Vesci family and were held from them by the Umfravilles who became the captains of Harbottle and, for a time, keepers of the Rede.

The Selby family are first recorded at Biddlestone in 1272 by a charter of King Henry III, later confirmed by Edward I. During the Scottish wars, the Selby family flourished as hard fighters; a member of the clan served as a governor of Liddell Castle in Roxburghshire and was executed for his pains. Another captured the King of Scots at Neville's Cross in Durham in 1346 and obtained a large share of his ransom, whilst yet another, William, was gentleman porter of the Castle of Berwick-on-Tweed during the reign of Elizabeth I. During the reign of James I and VI, five members of the Selby family were knighted by him, though this had more to do with the fees attached to the bestowal of that rank than anything else.

When Sir Walter Scott of Abbotsford visited Northumberland on one of his Border tours, he passed by Biddlestone Hall and used it (the 'old' hall; not that built in 1796) and the family as models for Osbaldistone Hall and Squire Osbaldistone in *Rob Roy*, though heavily caricatured. All of the Selbys in later generations were keen horsemen and foxhunters, as would be expected of landowners with extensive sheep grazings in the Border hills.

Biddlestone Chapel and Harden Hill

The last Selbys of Biddlestone died just before the Great War in 1914 when the estate and hall were sold to Farquhar Deuchar of Scottish and Tyneside Breweries. In 1951 the Biddlestone estate was sold again, and the hall was subsequently demolished. A private chapel, converted from a tower house in the last century, survives, and is now owned by a private trust which enables the sanctuary light to be kept burning, as it was over the centuries by that ancient Catholic family. When the estate was sold, the purchaser felled all of the valuable standing timber on the estate and then, it is alleged, he resold the farms to the sitting tenants for more than he paid for the whole property. The Biddle Stones, which are to be found to the south of the ruins of Biddle Stone Hall, are believed to be a pedestal and socket for a mediaeval market cross. This may have stood in the old village which was displaced when the new park to the front of Biddlestone Hall was enclosed. There is a theory that the Biddle Stones gave the area its name but, in most of the old existing documents relating to Biddlestone and the Selby family, the place is referred to as Biddlesdun or Biddlesden.

One of the more celebrated members of the Selby family was Prideaux John Selby of Twizel House, Warenford. This gentleman was a celebrated naturalist in the last century, reputedly having the finest collection of taxidermy in the north of England. He was also an early promoter of the railway line between Berwick and Newcastle before the rivers Tyne and Tweed were bridged.

CHAPTER EIGHT

CLENNEL

CLENNEL STANDS on a 'bonny haugh' or meadow on the banks of the River Alwin, just north of Alwinton. It was formerly the home of the Clennel family, but descended by marriage in the mid-18th century to the Wilkinsons, who lived there for the next 200 years. The old pele tower or bastle-house is part of the present mansion which was largely built in the Tudor style in 1895. It is now a holiday centre with chalets and caravans in the grounds.

In the early part of the present century, a lady member of the Wilkinson family married unwisely and against the wishes of her family. After a time she built a modern mansion just above Parsonside at Newton, called Wilkinson Park. She chose the site, it is said locally, so that she could look down upon her disapproving relatives!

Hard-by Clennel lies Clennel Street, an ancient green or drove road into the Bowmont Valley in Scotland. This route was in use even before the Romans came to Rochester and the traffic of livestock and goods - legal or otherwise - continued up and down it for centuries. The Alwin Haugh was another route, by which the monks of Newminster Abbey at Morpeth drove their flocks to summer on the hill grazings of Kidland before the Border Wars; it was a smugglers' route afterwards.

Clennel Hall and Grounds

In the mid-17th century there was a terrible feud between the Laird of Clennel and the Faw or Faa gang of gypsies. During the Middle Ages Johnny Faa was leader of a band of Border gypsies and styled himself 'Lord and Earle of Little Egypt'. He was considered so powerful that he was able to conclude a truce with King James IV of Scotland at Melrose, after terrorising the Borders. Wull (or Will) Faa was the last leader of power and substance during the 17th century, and his last direct descendant was crowned the last 'King of the Gypsies' at Yetholm before the beginning of this century. Even after the Union of the Crowns in 1603 the Borders were a wild, lawless locality. The gypsy band traded, mainly in horses, over a wide area, attending local horse fairs at Yetholm, Pennymuir, Jethart and Stagshaw, not to mention the ones farther afield such as Wigton, Dumfries and Appleby. Wull Faa's gang kidnapped the young heir of Clennel and, later, a daughter of the family. After a widespread fruitless search, Clennel gave up and returned home to a distraught wife. Some time later, however, whilst out hunting, Clennel's hounds overran a gypsy encampment. He then discovered to his horror that his hounds had mauled his long-lost daughter. Of his son, there was no sign. Many years later, return-  ing from fighting for Charles II and the defeated Royalists at the Battle of Worcester in 1651, Clennel was waylaid by an older man and a youth. After a struggle, Clennel was bound and taken to a gypsy encampment by the man, Wull Faa, and his own son, the youth. Old Elspeth Faa, the mother of Wull, forbade the execution of Clennel by his own son, and freed them both - much to the rage and chagrin of Wull Faa.

CHAPTER NINE

ALWINTON

THIS PARISH is one of the largest in England; it extends from the Scottish Border at Blindburn to Trewhitt and, at its broadest, stretches six miles from Makendon to the Farnhams. At its heart lies the village of Alwinton itself, sitting at the confluence of the rivers Alwin and Coquet. The river Coquet rises north of Alwinton, in the hills behind Makendon and Blindburn, to begin its 55-mile journey to the North sea at Amble. The river Alwin also rises in the Border line above Kidland Forest. Historically, Alwinton contained 11 townships and, at the more ancient site of Low Alwinton, sits the very pretty parish church of Saint Michael, with the Selby family vault in the chancel, and that of the Clennel family in the body of the church.

Otterburn military training range is close to Alwinton, occupying nearly 90 square miles or 60,000 acres. Here modern military training has co-existed with an extensive hill farming system of suckler cattle and hill sheep, very nicely, for almost a century. In previous centuries this same area was a military training ground for the Roman army manning Hadrian's Wall.

The Scottish-English border line was fixed by the commissioners of the two kingdoms at the Treaty of Northampton in 1328 which recognised the independence of Scotland and so allowed King Edward III to pursue his claims to the crown of France. It stayed in that fixed position, even after the Union of the Crowns in 1603 and the Union of the Parliaments in 1707. But in 1859 John Carr Esq, of Dunston in Co Durham and Hedgeley in Northumberland, who owned the hill grazings of Bygate Hall, Makendon, Loungesknow and Birdhope, discovered that a piece of land on his farm of Makendon called the Plea Shank - near to Russell's Cairn - had been included on the Scottish side of the border by the Ordnance Survey through a mistake on the part of their surveyor. After a lengthy battle in the courts, the Ordnance Survey had to admit defeat and redraw the map of the border; another blow struck for England - and without a drop of blood being shed!

Alwinton Border Shepherds' Show

The Border Shepherds' Show at Alwinton celebrated its 135th birthday in 1999. It is one of the three great border shows held every year for border folk and their friends. The others are Yetholm and Falstone. There are other village and community shows in Northumberland, but to win prizes for any commodity or class at these shows draws more honour and satisfaction than any of the premier national shows or exhibitions in either kingdom. The quality and number of entries in the sheep show and the industrial tent, along with the Cumberland wrestling and sports, as well as the hound trail, attract thousands of people each year.

Hound-trailing is a phenomenon peculiar to the Lakeland and Border hill areas. Grasmere is the original home of the hound- trailing sport. The specially bred trail-hounds are descendants of the slew-hounds, used to track humans during a Hot Trod (the pursuit of cattle raiders) in the Border Wars. At Alwinton these specially fed and trained hounds, whose body hair is shaved to ensure maximum speed, follow a drag of an aniseed mixture over a course of eight or ten miles. The drag is laid to enable spectators to view the whole race at all times. This also avoids any attempt at the trickery which used to be prevalent when huge sums of money were wagered on the outcome of the races.

River Alwin

Border sheep shows have evolved from the old gatherings, usually held twice yearly, when stray sheep were collected at a central point, and returned to their original owners. They were identified by the marks burnt into their horns or notched into their ears, and by various paint marks. These gatherings developed into a form of competition by shepherds and flockmasters anxious and interested to produce better stock than their neighbours. The degree of skill used preparing these animals for show would surprise even the most competent make-up artists in show business. This has its origin in the reiver's (raider's) skill in disguising animals so that even their own mothers and owners could not recognise them.

In the 20th century, Alwinton Show is bigger and more brash than the days of yore, when herds and flockmasters came, drank in the Rose and Thistle Inn, and slept it off in the neighbouring byre and stable before returning home, stone-cold sober and unshaven, four or five days later. The show is now more family orientated and, even if a 'few drams are taken', the showground gets tidied up next day and the village of Alwinton, at the heart of Upper Coquetdale, falls into a slumber until the second Saturday of October the following year.

Alwinton Sheep Show

CHAPTER TEN

ELSDON

Hae ye ivver been at Elsdon?
The world's unfinish'd neuk;
It stands amang the hungry hills
an' wears a frozen leuk.

AT SOME times of the year the rhyme would appear very appropriate, but Elsdon is a delightful spot and, in spite of its stormy past, a perfect example of the layout of a Border village. Its village green and the church of St Cuthbert are at its centre, while the houses and steadings encircle them in a defensive fashion, which was the original purpose of its existence - a place of safety from reivers and the lawless men of the borderland. Originally an important centre in if not the capital of Redesdale, it lost its pre-eminence when Harbottle Castle became the seat of governmental power in the 12th century. It remained, however, an important stopping point on the drove routes for the cattle trade and pack horses between the Scots and the English in later centuries. Consequently, there were quite a number of ale houses with the adjoining cock pit and bull baiting sites, as is still evident. The ale houses are now private dwellings and only the 'Bird in Bush' remains as a watering hole for the locals and visitors.

Elsdon Village and Church

The original motte and bailey castle earth work to the north- east is the oldest existing site in the village, but the rectory with its pele tower is the most impressive, originating - it is believed - towards the end of the 14th century. St Cuthbert's church was also largely constructed in that century on the site of an earlier church where it is believed that the bones of St Cuthbert rested on the long journey from Lindisfarne to Durham. There are marks on the pillars of the church where the inhabitants are thought to have sharpened their arrowheads and whetted the blades of their swords and daggers on the consecrated masonry. Excavations during the last century revealed the skeletal remains from mass burials alongside and inside the churchyard walls. These are reputed to be the fallen from the Battle of Otterburn, the culmination of the Scottish raid under Douglas through Elsdon in 1388, as the ballad of 'Chevy Chase' reminds us. The development of the turnpike road system, and what eventually became the A696, effectively bypassed the village. This meant that Otterburn became a more important port of call.

> *Over Ottercap' Hyll they came in,*
> *And so dowyn by Rodclyffe cragge,*
> *Upon Grene Leyton they lyghted dowyn,*
> *Styringe many a stagge.*
> *And boldely brente Northomberlond*
> *And haryed many a towyn;*

(Part of the old ballad 'The Battle of Otterburne')

'Winter's Gibbet' attracts the eye to the horizon just south and east of Elsdon. This was set up in 1791, and the body of William Winter was hung here, in chains, for the felony of robbery and murder. On the watershed where the gibbet stands is the remains of a much more interesting artefact: the Steng Cross, marked now only by a stone socket in the moss nearby. This must have been a landmark long before old Winter paid his price here. Near to the Steng Cross are the remains of an old smithy. Marked by four sycamore trees and some old buildings, this is where the cattle were actually shod with iron plates, similar to horses' shoes, to help them stand up to the long journeys on unmade roads into the midlands of England.

Famous family names abound still in Redesdale: Halls, Reeds, Robsons, Charltons, Milburns and Hedleys - one of whom, Thomas Hedley, born in Elsdon, migrated to Newcastle and founded the famous Thomas Hedley soap works which became part of the Proctor and Gamble multinational empire. Capability Brown's parents lived at Ravenscleugh where he was born, and their memorial stones are in Elsdon churchyard.

CHAPTER ELEVEN

ALNHAM

At the source of the River Aln lies the ancient hamlet of Alnham or 'Yeldom' as it was called in former times.

For Yeldomites are strong and bold,
They can stand the heat as well as the cold;
When once they grip they keep their hold,
Whatever ye may try.

T HE RIVER Aln rises in Hazeltonrig Wood, a large plantation south and west of a hill fort on Castle Hill. This ancient settlement's ramparts and circles are similar to those elsewhere in the Cheviot foothills. The Church of St Michael the Archangel at Alnham formerly belonged to the White (Premonstratensian) Canons of Alnwick Abbey, though there must have been a church on the site long before their arrival in the 12th century. The churchyard is still in use although graves are difficult to excavate without disruption of earlier interments. The church itself has needed restoration on at least five occasions, the last thanks to the late Major Gus Renwick of Holystone, whose woods supplied the timber for its re-roofing and for building the charming lych-gate, as well as supplying the sinews of restoration, i.e. cash. The old vicarage, which incorporates an even older pele tower, did service as a youth hostel before becoming a private residence in the last decades of this century.

Alnham Church and Vicar's Pele

Alnham suffered largely from the depradations of the Scots and in 1349 it was visited by the plague brought, it is said, in a bundle of washing to the vicarage. In 1587, the Bold Buccleuch launched a revenge raid down the valleys of the Coquet, Breamish and the Aln - burning, stealing and slaying - prompting the then proprietor, the Earl of Northumberland, to complain to King Henry VIII. 'Scots, to the numbre of 300, hathe brunte a toune of mine called Alenham, with all the corne, hay and household stuff in the said toune, and also a woman.' In more modern times Alnham, with its 'tofts and crofts' and the enclosure of Alnham Common, became one of the great sheep farming areas of Northumberland. In the early 19th century Dr Anthony Marshall of Chatton Park and his brother-in-law Adam Atkinson of Alnham and Lorbottle took advantage of the Highland Clearances to send flocks of sheep from the Borders into the Highlands of Scotland, creating great fortunes for themselves as graziers.

Whittingham Vale has always had another passion apart from whisky; that is a love of the horse - racing, hunting and breeding. The late Adam Scott of Alnham (son of Sir Henry Scott of Hipsburn, owner of Bolsover Collieries in Derbyshire, and a grazier in Inverness-shire and the Isle of Skye) was one of the great horsemen of his time. On the broad Alnham acres, he bred and raced his own horses, wearing his own sky-blue silks and a claret-coloured cap. He met his death at Kelso racecourse riding his own horse 'Command' in 1925 and is buried in his colours in Alnham churchyard. His other prominent racehorses were 'Jazzband', which won the Pitman's Derby in 1924 as well as other prestigious races, and 'Ruritania' which won the Scottish Grand National. Others were 'Oriel', 'Wildfire', 'Westwood' and his favourite 'Black Ivory'.

At the time of the Boer War, Sir Henry Scott (Adam Scott's father) offered 1,000 guineas and his son, Adam, to the government of the day to form one of the first regiments of Imperial Yeomanry, and his offer was gratefully accepted. Adam Scott eventually ended up as a galloper (i.e. dispatch rider) for General Sir John French. He is reputed to have galloped his horse over a pedestrian trestle-bridge escaping from his Boer pursuers, and was mentioned in dispatches for this feat.

Other longstanding tenants of the Alnham farms have been the Sordy family, ducal tenants for centuries at Warkworth and Alnwick as well as Alnham. Harry Sordy came to farm there in 1934 and farmed the extensive hill grazings there for nearly 50 years. An outstanding stockbreeder and farmer, his great love was for his horses. He was reputed to have the best 'hands' in England; his skill and expertise with horses in the hunting and racing field was legendary. As a youth he was meant to train with Adam Scott as a jockey, and after Scott's death he rode many of Scott's horses as well as others,winning among other trophies the Heart of All England trophy at Hexham, and the John Peel Cup in Cumberland. Among the horses at Alnham during this period ridden by Harry was the grey gelding 'Bandra' owned by the Green family and a winner of the Scottish Grand National. Others of his great performers on the turf were 'Barricade' and 'Black Chesters'.

Towards the end of the Second World War, Hugh, the young 10th Duke of Northumberland, decided to cross the Border and ask for the hand in marriage of the young Lady Elizabeth Montagu-Douglas-Scott, daughter of Walter, 9th Duke of Buccleuch and 13th Duke of Queensberry. Harry Sordy arranged the horses and the guide for the Duke, one of the Alnham shepherds, Wattie Little, from an old border riding family who herded one of the highest hirsels at Alnham. Little, as a foxhunting man, knew all of the passages and byways in the Border hills. He safely guided his charge on horseback and delivered him to Bowhill near Selkirk where the question was popped and the agreement was settled. The wedding of the head of the house of Hotspur and a daughter of the house of the 'Bold' Buccleuch was celebrated in Westminster Abbey in 1946 in the presence of King George VI and Queen Elizabeth, thus officially ending the Border feud which began 700 years previously - and they all lived happily ever after.

Alnham village hall was built in 1919 to commemorate the fallen of the Great War. The site and the stone were donated by the 8th Duke of Northumberland; the carting of materials was done by villagers and farmworkers of the parish, as was the labouring - all in their own free time - and the construction was paid for by public subscription raised locally. The roll of honour of this terrible conflict lists seven dead and 19 who served, out of a population of 115 souls, including men, women and children.

The Cheviot foothills have always had a reputation for stormy weather, often blowing up at short notice, with strong blizzards and deep snowdrifts. In 1962, two of the Alnham shepherds returning home from a late November sheep sale at Rothbury were overcome by storm conditions and lost their lives at Gappeth which was not very far from their home at Ewartly Shank. Almost a century before this, a young woman walking from Hartside, Linhope to Alnham was overcome by storm and lost her life at Cobden Old Walls, near to Prendwick Chesters. 'Nellie Heron's stone' still marks the spot where her body was found.

CHAPTER TWELVE

LEMMINGTON AND EDLINGHAM

EDLINGHAM WAS a Saxon homestead which developed into a substantial settlement and was one of the four Northumbrian royal villages given to St Cuthbert by King Ceolwulf when he resigned his throne to become a monk on Lindisfarne. The Roman road known as the Devil's Causeway passes near here and there are plenty of cup-and-ring marked stones on the hills to the south, proving that the area was occupied long before the Saxon era. The church of St John the Baptist was originally attached to Tynemouth Priory, the daughter house of the great monastery of St Albans, and during the time of the Reformation was reckoned to be a harbour for 'pestiferous traitors and inciters of the people', papists. The castle of Edlingham for centuries was used as a source of stone for building. Originally a hall house, its defences were added when it was licensed to be crenellated at the outbreak of the Scottish Wars in 1296. The archaeological excavations of recent years (1978-1982) have added much to our knowledge of buildings and life during the medieval period. The estate of Edlingham came via marriage to the Swinburne family of Capheaton who held it until the early part of the 20th century.

The Rothbury to Alnwick road south of the village was built in 1754 and is called 'The Corn Road'. This route conveyed grain and wool from central Northumberland to the then important port of Alnmouth. This road was promoted in the greater part by Launcelot Allgood of Nunwick, who also promoted the military road constructed by Field Marshal Wade from Newcastle to Carlisle between the two Jacobite rebellions of 1715 and 1745. Plague visited Edlingham in the middle of the 17th century and the farm of Newtown dates from this period.

Edlingham Castle and Village

There was a notorious case of witchcraft at Edlingham in 1683 when one Alexander Nichol of Lorbottle alleged that his child had died as a result of Margaret Stothard of Edlingham applying a spell. Nichol's wife alleged that Stothard had asked for alms but was refused. She went on to claim that the child said that Margaret Stothard 'did wave at her mother a white thing three times'; next morning the child grew unwell and died shortly after, during this time crying out that '... the woman who waved the white thing at you is pressing of me and is leike to bricke my backe and press out my hart...'. Another accusation against Margaret Stothard was raised by John Mills of Edlingham, alleging that she materialised in his bedroom at his bedfoot only to disappear when he exclaimed, 'the witch, the witch'. These depositions were made to a local JP, Mr Ogle of Eglingham Hall and Lady Widdrington, Squiress of Cartington, but there seems to be no record of Margaret Stothard's apprehension or punishment. She appears to have been an itinerant and may have been part of the large gypsy population which lived in the Borders and rural Northumberland during the 16th and 17th centuries. Another such was the infamous Meg of Meldon who was married to a member of the Fenwick clan and was believed to practice witchcraft.

More recently, in the 19th century, there was the infamous Edlingham burglary. The vicarage was robbed by two armed men; two well-known poachers were subsequently arrested and convicted for the offence and sentenced to penal servitude. These unfortunate men were pardoned after ten years' incarceration when two others confessed to the crime.

The Manor of Lemmington, close to Edlingham, probably originated as a Saxon vill. It certainly formed part of the barony of Beanley, which was held by the Cospatrick Earls of Northumberland under the feudal terms of Grand Sargenty until Henry Percy, Lord of Alnwick, obtained the barony at the beginning of the 14th century. The Manor of Lemmington, however, was later attached to the barony of Shawdon, and over the years it changed hands between Herons and Fenwicks and Ogles until the Hargrave-Pawson family purchased it in the 18th century. The most historic parts of Lemmington still existing are the old pele tower, which is almost completely enclosed by the present mansion house, and the old garden wall built of Dutch brick brought over from Holland as ballast in empty vessels coming to ship grain during the time of the French wars of Louis XIV. Another interesting feature not readily seen are the cultivation terraces to the east of the present mansion house. For many years it was assumed that these were of mediaeval origin. Recent archeological work, however, is beginning to suggest that they could even go back to Roman times.

Edlingham Church

The mansion house at Lemmington has been allowed to fall into disrepair many times over the centuries; the first house was built by Nicholas Fenwick (a merchant of Newcastle) sometimes mistaken for, but in fact related to, Alderman Fenwick of Newcastle. Much of the interior of that mansion was removed by the Hargrave-Pawsons to re-build and refurbish Titlington Hall at the beginning of the 19th century and it was not until the present century that Sir Stephen Aitchison, the wealthy merchant grocer from Tyneside, began to re-build it in its present form. He purchased many fixtures and fittings at the demolition of Camelford House in London and transported them to Lemmington. Within the park at Lemmington is the Evelyn Monument, first erected in 1783 by Edward and Julia Evelyn at Felbridge Place, East Grinstead, Surrey and designed by Sir John Soane, the architect of the Bank of England. In 1928, with building development impending at Felbridge, the monument was bought by Sir Stephen Aitchison for re-erection in his park.

When Sir Stephen Aitchison bought the Lemmington estate, the area surrounding Lemmington Hall was a barren, treeless landscape, but over the next 30 years he planted many trees, including many specimen varieties - corsican pine, silver fir, beech and sycamore - which still remain there today. The Cecil Rhodes oak tree was grown - it is said - from an acorn presented by Rhodes to a member of the Aitchison family and planted, according to its stone marker, in 1907. There are also many sequoia (inland gigantica) standing individually and in groups; this magnificent variety originated in California. East of the Hall is an avenue of western red cedar, the stone marker of which - inscribed in Latin - indicates that these were also planted in 1907. At the far western end of the policies is the old quarry, the sandstone from which was used to build the original Hall and its outbuildings. The quarry was once an attractive wild garden, but is now overgrown. The 'rhododendron walk' was a feature, connecting the front of the Hall to the western edge of the gardens, opening out to a vista overlooking Edlingham towards Winter Coe.

At the end of World War II Sir Walter Aitchison, who lived at Copeland Castle near Wooler, offered the use of Lemmington Hall to the Roman Catholic Diocese of Hexham and Newcastle, at the suggestion of one of his store managers. In 1947 the first Sisters of the Sacred Heart of Jesus and Mary arrived to begin their devoted work of nursing and supporting ladies in their care, which went on for almost 50 years.

Lemmington Hall and the Evelyn Monument

There is an ancient legend concerning Lemmington and the tale goes like this:

Upon a midsumer night in a bygone age when ye good and moste vertuous Ladye Queen Egfrya of ye lande of Northumbria, having lived one hundred and foure years of hir devoute life, was passing ye nocturnal houres in solente contemplacion by ye founte of Lemyngtonne Halle, there came to hir a vision of ye Queen among Faeries.

Quoth she unto Egfrya:
Good Ladye I come to bestowe a favor. Thus far an hundred requests have I granted unto thee. Now at ye ende of thy life, in thy one hundred and fourth year, I wolde bestowe one other favour. Good Ladye, prithee speak.

Spake Egfrya thus:
Fayre Queen, no thing is wanting unto me. But for a benefitte unto my fellows I wolde request that to all who shalle cast but one silver coyne in yonder founte of Lemyngtonne a wish shalle be fulfilled.

Quoth ye Queen of Faeries:
Thus shalle it be.

The site of this 'founte' has never been found.

CHAPTER THIRTEEN

CHILLINGHAM

CHILLINGHAM CASTLE was the centre of one of the great feudal estates of Northumberland, stretching from the coastline south of Craster to Cornhill-on-Tweed, and including most of the ancient Forest of Cheviot. At its zenith the property embraced many thousands of acres and included scores of manors and villages, and hundreds of farms and hamlets.

The castle itself has served as a border fortress of some importance, being visited by several monarchs including Henry III and Edward I. Latterly, Edward VII came in 1872 when he was Prince of Wales. With the coming of the Grey family to Chillingham in the 13th century, the castle was further strengthened and then fortified in 1344, and both family and castle played a major role in the Scottish and Border wars.

With the Union of the Crowns, the castle was turned into a more gracious family dwelling, with many extensions and improvements made over the next 300 years. The castle is widely regarded as one of the best examples of a fortified domestic building. For most of the 20th century it has been empty, and it suffered much from occupation by the Army during World War II. Recently, a programme of restoration has started to reveal many of its ancient secrets and it has begun to regain some of its former glory. As might be expected, the castle is haunted. The 'Radiant Boy' or 'Blue Boy' is the most notorious ghost. It is not known who he was but local legend has it that the bones of a child were discovered built into the wall of a bedroom he haunted. Other phantoms are reputed to have been seen over the years by inhabitants and locals.

Chillingham Castle

The parish church of Saint Peter at Chillingham is one of the most delightful places of worship in this part of the world. Originally part of the foundation of Alnwick Abbey (confirmed by a document dated 1348) the church is undoubtedly of Norman origin but the site would almost certainly have been a place of worship prior to this.

This church contains the magnificent tomb of Sir Ralph Grey (d.1443) and his wife Elizabeth. It is carved in fine sandstone and alabaster, and supports the effigies of Sir Ralph and his wife; around the top of the tomb are carved the badges of the Greys - all ladders and cloaks, the ancient emblems of this Norman-French family ('gre' being Norman-French for 'ladder'). It is believed that the tomb-chest was brought from Scotland, carved by workmen under the Parisian craftsman Jean Moreau, head mason and architect at Melrose Abbey.

In 1997, whilst on a visit to Alnwick Castle, the present Prince of Wales visited the church unobserved by anyone, though he signed the visitors' book. His hope was to see the wild cattle - like his great-great-grandfather in the last century - but he was unable to find them.

There are many interesting and curious memorials in the church and churchyard. The Charnocke monument relates to Robert Charnocke, a former steward of the Chillingham Estates at the time of Forde, Lord Grey of Chillingham, who was attainted for treason because of his involvement in the Monmouth rebellion of 1685, when his estates were confiscated. His faithful steward forestalled the collection of rents by the Earl of Rochester's men, by collecting them himself and sending them to his master in exile in Holland.

A most curious headstone dated 1771 near the churchyard gate reads:

My friends go home
& cease from tears
I must ly hear til Christ
A peares

Chillingham Castle and Gardens

There also used to be a plague stone in the churchyard: a hollowed-out stone into which vinegar was poured allowing the alms and offerings to be steeped in the liquid for purification before collection. Plague visited the area in 1665.

The vast Chillingham Estates were a collection of manors and fiefs gathered together over the centuries by marriage, inheritance, purchase and conquest, and held by a strong right arm. Until the latter half of the 18th century subsistence farming, fishing and barter economy operated. But in 1785, John Bailey of Barnard Castle was appointed Steward of Chillingham by Charles, 5th Earl of Tankerville. Bailey was one of the foremost agriculturalists and administrators of his day and promoted the development of the estate by the regularising of farm tenancies with long-term, formal leases, the clearance and enclosure of wastes and commons and the introduction of new capitalist tenant farmers. Bailey was reputed to have increased the rent roll of the estates from £14,000 to over £100,000 in the 35 years of his stewardship.

One of his more successful tenant families were the Culleys, from Durham, who were great livestock breeders and farmers. In 1810 John Bailey and George Culley collaborated in writing a report on the state of farming in Northumberland (*General View of the Agriculture of the County of Northumberland*) for the Board of Agriculture, whose president was Sir John Sinclair of Caithness, one of the prime movers of agricultural improvement in the late 18th and early 19th centuries. Another great national agricultural improver who had charge of the Chillingham Estates was Sir Jacob Wilson KCVO. Appointed Steward in 1865 by Charles, 6th Earl of Tankerville, Wilson was the son of a tenant farmer, originally from Cumberland but then a tenant of, and agent for, the Cresswell family at Woodhorn near Cresswell. He was educated at Cirencester, the Royal Agricultural College, and farmed with his father as well as looking after the Cresswell family land holdings until his appointment at Chillingham. He was a director of the Land Division and Agricultural Advisor to the Board of Agriculture, a founder member of the Royal Forestry Society and Honorary Director of the Royal Agricultural Society, and was responsible for the very first Royal Agricultural Shows in the last century.

Chillingham Church

Chillingham Lake

Glendale and Cheviot foothills (panorama)

Hepburn Bastle and Chillingham Park (panorama continued)

A visit to Chillingham would not be complete without trying to see the wild cattle. These famous beasts are reputed to have been pure bred since ancient times, with no other outcross with any other breeds. Certainly the park has been enclosed since mediaeval times and they breed true to type on every occasion. Over the centuries the herd has suffered many vicissitudes. During the Border Wars but after the park was enclosed, and again during the Civil War period (1654), Scottish troops decimated it . In 1689 William Taylor, the steward, reported that the herd had been reduced to 16 'white wilde beasts'. In 1932 at the final break-up of the Chillingham estates, the trustees agreed to lease the park to an Association which would look after the future of the herd, at this time numbering 44 cattle. The herd nearly died out in the big snowstorm of 1947 when its numbers fell to the lowest ebb. Another challenge to its security came in 1965, the year of the disastrous foot-and-mouth outbreak in Northumberland; a nearby outbreak of the disease nearly caused the slaughter of the whole herd. Since then a reserve herd has been established at a secret location in Scotland - thought to be in the region of the Ancient Forest of Caledonia - from where it is believed these animals originated. The park at Chillingham is now owned by the Sir James Knott Trust, and is administered by College Valley Estates - also owned by the trustees - who have opened up considerable areas of the park to public access. These arrangements ensure a safe future for the herd.

Near the ruins of Hepburn Bastle, just outside Chillingham Park walls, lies Hepburn Wood. This Forestry Commission plantation has several walks cut through it which allow fine views of the Cheviots. There is also a stone dedicated to Fritz Berthele, who planted many of the trees here.

Within the grounds of Chillingham Castle stands a very fine equestrian statue of Field Marshal Hugh, Viscount Gough GCB, GCSI, an Irishman who served in the Peninsular War against the French and later in China and India. Although, in the words of fellow-general Sir Charles Napier, 'as brave as ten lions, each with two sets of teeth and two tails', Gough's victories against the Sikhs in the 1840s were very bloody affairs because he was so averse to using his artillery to soften up the enemy. The statue, cast from guns taken by troops under his command, stood for many years in Dublin. It was discovered in a scrapyard after it had been blown up by the IRA during the present troubles.

CHAPTER FOURTEEN

FORD

FORD WAS originally part of the barony of Wooler, bestowed upon Robert Muschamp by Henry I - that able son of the Conqueror - who created a series of baronies in Northumberland to provide a buffer zone against the Scots. The manor of Ford over the years was occupied by the Heron and Carr families. The first castle at Ford was built by Sir William Heron in 1287 as a defence against the depredations of the Scots, but was taken and demolished by them in 1385. It is probably best known for the part that it played in the preliminaries to the Battle of Flodden, which was fought in the next-door parish of Branxton. It was here that King James IV of Scotland paid court to the beautiful daughter of Sir William Heron, while he was a prisoner in Scotland. It is said that her mother encouraged this liaison in order to distract the king whilst the English forces assembled in greater strength and then outmanoeuvered his army. In 1998 Branxton Hill, the site of Flodden Field, resembled a sea of yellow as a result of the oilseed rape grown here; only the monument, which marks the spot of the death of the Scottish king on Pipers Hill, stood out. On that fateful day in 1513 the landscape would also have been a sea of yellow - but of broom in full bloom.

Beside Branxton is a brook; breathless they lie
Gaping against the moon: their ghosts went away.

(from a Border Ballad)

Ford Castle and Church

In 1717 the Delaval family inherited the estate and manor of Ford, and in 1761 Sir John Hussey Delaval (later raised to the peerage) commenced rebuilding the castle and developing his estate. He employed his considerable wealth in enclosure and cultivation. In addition, he introduced a plating mill and forge, as well as developing his coal mines on Ford Common. On his death in 1808 the estate passed to his widow for her lifetime, and on her death in 1822, the property passed to her granddaughter Susan, Marchioness of Waterford.

The modern Ford Castle owes much to the Marchioness who came to live here on being widowed in 1859. She again rebuilt much of the castle, as well as Ford village, creating a school, smithy, reading-room and dairy; in other words, a model village. One of Lady Waterford's most outstanding contributions lies in the village hall - which used to be the village school - where her mural paintings (in fact, watercolours on paper) have recently been restored. She used village people as models, some of whose descendants still live in the area. Among the flow of distinguished visitors whom Lady Waterford entertained at Ford was John Ruskin who, on seeing her paintings, made the rather churlish remark, 'I thought that you would have done something better'.

The grey stone bridge at Ford over the river Till was the most convenient crossing between the Doddington and Twizel bridges in the past when smuggling was rife. Whisky, distilled in Scotland, could be bought in carts loaded with corn through the toll bar on the bridge with impunity, whilst the disused shafts and pitfalls of Ford Common made useful hiding places for the contraband. The return trips were usually of Holland gin and French brandy landed at Seahouses and Boulmer, as the old rhyme goes:

Aad Jimmy Turner of Ford, did not think it a sin
To saddle his horse on a Sunday and ride to Boulmer for gin.

Salt was another commodity for smuggling, usually hidden beneath loads of clotted lime from Lowick or under cartloads of coal from Ford Common.

Lady Waterford Hall and Ford Village

In 1907 the Waterford family sold the estate and castle of Ford to the first Lord Joicey. During the agricultural depression of the 1930s, a young local shepherd, wishing to get married but unable to find a job with a house, approached Lord Hugh Joicey at his estate office at Ford. He was dressed for hunting and about to leave, but asked the young man to come back next day, which he duly did with his request to rent a cottage somewhere with a bit of 'rabbit catching'. Lord Joicey studied his references and said, 'Yes, I can let you have somewhere to live, and some rabbit catching, but you must take the tenancy of the farm with it'! The young man took the tenancy on, and his grandson still farms on the estate today.

Ford Forge and Heatherslaw Mill

CHAPTER FIFTEEN

ETAL

ETAL, LIKE Ford, was another manor of the barony of Wooler, held in service by the Manners family for 'half a knight's fee'. The castle was built to guard an important ford over the river Till and, consequently, was a target for many a Scots raiding party. The Manners family were supporters of both sides during the Wars of the Roses but, finally, in 1495, George Manners of Etal inherited titles and lands in Rutland where the family eventually became Dukes of Rutland. In 1547, the family exchanged lands at Etal with the Crown for further lands in Rutland.

The castle at Etal was taken by the Scots in 1513 just before Flodden. Damage then, and subsequent lack of maintenance, left it in a ruinous state. Etal eventually passed to the Carr family who built the manor house (1748) at the east end of the village. The last member of the Carr family, Lady Augusta - who married Lord Frederick Fitzclarence, an illegitimate son of King William IV - lived at Etal for a number of years. Lord Fitzclarence placed the pair of naval cannon, salvaged from the wreck of HMS *Royal George*, at the gateway to the castle, where they remain.

The village of Etal, with its picturesque, thatch-roofed inn and tidy gardens, is one of the most attractive in Northumberland. Now the property of the Joicey family, who bought the estate in 1908, the village is being developed tastefully to support the tourist industry. The estate has laid out a narrow-gauge model railway along the banks of the river Till and, under the guardianship of English Heritage, a new museum and associated facilities have been established around the old castle.

Etal Castle and Flodden Field

Bamburgh Castle and Farne Islands from Ross Links

Lindisfarne from Guile Point on Ross Links – oyster beds bottom left

CHAPTER SIXTEEN

LINDISFARNE

THE LINDISFARNE National Nature Reserve stretches from Cheswick Sands to Budle Bay. It encompasses the Fenham Flats and the Ross Back Sands, Goswick Beach and Lindisfarne or Holy Island. It is one of the most important international wildfowl wintering habitats in the world. Shelduck, lapwing, eider, wigeon, redshank, bar-tailed godwit, curlew and greylag all over-winter here on the mud-flats, which provide essential food for these waterfowl.

In the past, Holy Island - apart from being one of the cradles of Christianity in England - has served, with its castle, as a military outpost. The Lordship of the Manor of Holy Island is vested in the Crossman family of Cheswick who acquired the estate in the last century. Until recently the main source of employment and income has been through the island's farms and fishing. In the 18th century limestone was quarried here and the burnt lime was exported to Dundee. The massive kilns near the castle are evidence of this industry. Since the establishment of the causeway, opening up the island to the motor car, the tourist industry in its season provides the most income, employment, and headaches.

Lindisfarne Priory

In May 1643, during the English Civil War, a squadron of ships from the Parliamentarian navy received the subjection of Berwick and the same evening landed 100 soldiers. Captain Richard Haddock, commander of the squadron, reported to his masters in London that they 'marched to Colonel Haggerston of Haggerston Castle [opposite Lindisfarne] … The Colonel which we have taken had like to have made an easy escape, for at our first entrance into the Castle, he slipped out at a back door, but being espied by the soldiers, they fired four muskets at him … shot his man through the boot top, but killed neither of them. Both he and his son were newly come from the Earl of Newcastle's [the Royalist commander in the North of England] army, and were then raising a regiment of horse for his service. That night there were seven troops of horse within two miles of the Castle, which he knew not of, but I wonder how they could forbear laughing the next morning when they came to hear their captain snapped up by a ship. We had no sooner brought them to our boat … but down came his troop to the sea-side (our ship riding a mile and a half from the shore) where sitting on horseback, they discharged their pistols at us.' A few days later, on May 29, he turned his attention to Lindisfarne Castle. After a preliminary cannonade, one Rugg, the Captain of the castle, agreed to yield on condition that he and his men were paid the year's wages they were owed and which had never been paid by their Royalist masters.

Lindisfarne Castle

At the beginning of this century Edward Hudson, the founder of *Country Life* magazine, bought the castle, now owned by the National Trust, and had it restored by Sir Edwin Lutyens, later to design the viceregal city of New Delhi in India. Hudson also employed the famous gardener, Gertrude Jekyll, to design and construct a garden. This was envisaged as a summer garden and was to contain gladioli, roses, hollyhocks, fuschias, mallows, sunflowers and Japanese anemones. In addition to this in 1911 she ordered from Suttons Seeds - potatoes, peas, spinach, dwarf beans, parsley, carrots, cabbage, cauliflower, lettuce, beet and onions, whilst Messrs Barrs Nurseries supplied plants of mint, thyme, sage, sorrel, chives and savoury.

O for a pea in a purple pod;
For this I labour and turn the sod;
And trench it deep for many a rod;
And carry manure in a bricklayer's hod;
All for a pea in a purple pod.

This was written on a train journey to Newcastle by Gertrude Jekyll. Among the natural vegetation on Holy Island is the very attractive henbane which, unfortunately, is very poisonous to humans and, in fact, is the weed with which Dr Crippen is alleged to have poisoned his wife.

A little-known local tale concerns a military training exercise held on Holy Island prior to D-Day. General Montgomery was overseeing troop-training exercises with the use of beach landing craft attacking Holy Island. Among the defenders of the Island was a local platoon of the Home Guard who were marooned on the island for twelve hours before the attack by the tides. Given the plethora of public houses, they proceeded to get gloriously drunk and were unable to defend or even welcome the invading troops, much to the General's chagrin, who disbanded them.

Lindisfarne Castle Garden

Slightly to the south and west of Holy Island, but part of the mainland, is Ross Farm, once regarded as an important rabbit warren, when these animals, along with pigeons, formed part of the staple diet. At high tide, because of the Ross Slakes to the north and Budle Bay to the south, it almost becomes an island. It was once part of the Tankerville estate, and there used to be an oysterman there whose job was to catch and supply oysters for Chillingham Castle. The oysterman lived in a little lodge beside the beacons (which guide and warn seaborne traffic) and he used a pony and trap to transport his catch to the castle kitchens. This custom died out about 100 years ago but recently a new venture in oyster farming started up and successfully markets its produce far and wide. The fact that the oysters live and thrive is a very good natural indicator of the purity of the waters in this area.

At the southern side of Budle Bay, which was once an important port for the shipment of grain, is the home of the legendary Laidly (or Loathsome) Worm, which is said to have terrorised the locality in similar circumstances to the Lambton Worm, before being slain by 'Childe Harold'.

Lindisfarne

Budle Bay (panorama)

Budle Bay (panorama continued)

EPILOGUE

Northumberland is no longer a grass county; it is largely arable, but there are still major stock-rearing areas, especially in the uplands, where sheep increasingly compete with the red grouse and sitka spruce. In recent years on some parts of the Cheviot massif there has been work going on to improve habitat to help the restoration of the blackcock. This is done under the auspices of the 'Black Game Project' organised and financed by some private landowners and some other outside agencies.

The colliery waste heaps which until fifty years ago dominated south-east-Northumberland – and which, incidentally, harboured a wide variety of bird and insect life, flora and fauna around the fringes – have now been landscaped, and the new plantations are beginning to be recolonised by many of the species which disappeared while this massive reclamation scheme was going on. Even the recently landscaped areas which have followed large-scale opencast mining are beginning to blend in and to support an increasingly varied range of birds and other wildlife.

In spite of the influence of modern agriculture there are still parts of Northumberland where large flocks of curlews make their landfall before they migrate to the uplands of the county for their breeding and nesting season. Similarly, in other parts of Northumberland and, strangely enough, especially on the War Department ranges between Redesdale and Alwinton, you can still hear the lark, often alongside the thunder of modern weaponry.

Even though man sometimes uses his environment harshly, nature has a way of adapting and reasserting itself. And in spite of man's addiction to electronic gadgetry, the ancient oral traditions and folklore still survive.